SALT AND LIGHT

SALT AND LIGHT

Poems by
KENNETH STEVEN

SAINT ANDREW PRESS

First published in 2007 by
SAINT ANDREW PRESS
121 George Street
Edinburgh EH2 4YN

Copyright © Kenneth Steven, 2007

ISBN 978 0 7152 0842 7

British Library Cataloguing in Publication Data
A catalogue record for this book is available from the British Library

It is the Publisher's policy to only use papers that are natural and recyclable and that have been manufactured from timber grown in renewable, properly managed forests. All of the manufacturing processes of the papers are expected to conform to the environmental regulations of the country of origin.

Typeset by Waverley Typesetters, Fakenham
Printed and bound in the United Kingdom by Bell & Bain Ltd, Glasgow

CONTENTS

Poems in this collection have been published by:

Acumen, *The Antigonish Review* (Canada), *Caduta Arts Review*, *Chapman*, *The Christian Science Monitor* (US), *Coracle*, *The Countryman*, *Dreamcatcher*, *Envoi*, *Essence*, *The Fireside Book*, the *Herald*, *Life & Work*, *The London Magazine*, *Markings*, *The Merton Journal*, *Northwords Now*, *New Writing Scotland*, *Offshoots* (Switzerland), *Poetry Scotland*, *Planet*, *Poetry Wales*, *Pulsar*, *Scintilla*, *The Scots Magazine*, *Staple*, *South* and *The Reader*.

'Seeing' was read by the author on BBC Radio 4's 'Poetry Please'.

DEDICATION

Books tend to be dedicated to one or a number of individuals. When I came to swirl together the poems for this collection, I immediately knew that three written in Michigan would have to find places among its pages. I then decided that here was an ideal opportunity to dedicate the volume to the very special friends I've made in the state, and to thank them for all their kindness and generosity of spirit. How often do I wish the water between here and there weren't quite so wide.

❖ LIGHT

Once upon a time it was carried
Fluttering, out of the caves.
The eyes gathered,
Wide with wonder, oiled with the flicker
Of reflected flame. The man who found it
Fed it, twig by twig, tenderly,
Mothering that orange play of light
(Like hands in a mime too quick to read).

He carried it that night over water,
Across the marsh thigh-deep in blackness,
Carried it high as his head,
Wading the treacle water, the others
Anxious about him, watching, wary
In the ghost breath of the dark.

Yet the flicker lived, was cradled
Onto the far side, into their future,
This thing that leapt out of flint
From the dry chisel of stone, this spirit
Mystical, bigger than themselves.

They made him king, the man who brought the light;
They made him a band of melted gold.

THE BEEHIVE CELLS

What drove their feet to these scree islands
Scarcely more than whalebacks in the sea,
To build shale haystacks under one huge grey wind,
To spend their dust of years huddled in the keen
Of sleet and rain on islands gnawed to knucklebones
Of winter gale? Nothing but this flint of faith
That lit a single flickering of lamp, and the sun
That after dark burst big and orange, beautiful
Through morning, sometimes, to everything the
    heart.

◈ CLONMACNOISE

Wrapped in the wool of winter
The fields breathed with frost

Even the Shannon confused
Searching in ribbons through the fields

The sun straining to see
Like a single frozen eye

We came to Clonmacnoise
Fifteen hundred years too late

Crows in the ivied silence of round towers
Gravestones bent as though in penitence

Chapels fallen in upon themselves
Like broken faith

And yet I could imagine
In the once upon a time of Ireland

Men awakening to break the wells
To bring in steamings of white water

Keeping the turf fire's glow
Storm after December storm

Here where they had caught God's light
(So fragile, yet alive for ever)

To bear it bright
Out into the dark places of the earth

▨ COLUMBA

It was another day. The bell echoed,
A coracle came with news of Ireland
And a fine cut of meat. The sea
Wrapped round the island like a mantle of silk.

Everything he did as always, just a beat slower.
They saw nothing; the talk was generous,
The laughter easy, as a lark spun songs
Somewhere out of sky that still morning.

Yet the horse came. In the middle of it all,
And the faces turned like full moons
As that long head rested on his shoulder
And the nostrils, full of hay, flared.

For the horse had heard
Dark in the drumbeat of his heart
That edge of death, and wept
Softly against the old man's head.

Salt tears like the water that had brought him once
Out of the heart of Ireland,
That would take him now
Over a last sea, into the land he had lived.

THE ILLUMINATED MANUSCRIPT

They brought me here from Ireland, still a boy
To begin their book.

I remember the day I left –
Soft bread, a silvering of geese, the sound of my
    mother.

Now I slip the stone of these steps every day
Long before dawn, breathe the dark

And hear the whelming of the winds about this
    fastness
Before my one candle like a petal of gorse

Flutters the shadows in ghosts over the cold walls.
Out of the thin window I watch the sea all winter

Heave and drag like a dying man,
The skies blackened and bruised.

Some days there is nothing in the pen except
My own emptiness; I hold it hoping

Until the stars blow out from the attic of the skies
And a ledge of moon lifts across the hills.

Just sometimes something breaks inside
Like the brittle lid of a casket

And pours out light onto the waiting page.

❖ IONA FERRY

It's the smell I remember –
The dizziness of diesel, tarry rope, wood sheened
    like toffee.
The sea was waving in the wind, a dancing –
I wanted it to be rough and yet I didn't.
My mother and I snugged under the awning,
To a dark rocking. We were as low as the waves,
All of us packed in tight like bales of wool.

The engine roared alive, its tremor
Juddered through the wood and thrilled me, beat
    my heart.
The shore began fading behind the white curl of our
    hum.
Fourteen days lay barefoot on the island –
Still asleep, their eyes all shut.
And yet I knew them all already,
Felt them in my pocket like polished stones –
Their orchids, their hurt-white sand, their larksong.

◈ THE COLOURISTS

They came out here in the first years of the century,
Their eyes still drunk on Paris and Venice –
Here to the edge of the world, this blowing place,
Where the days are a constant gale,
Where everything is always changing
In a flurry of bright gusts.

They came out here
To put easels into the north wind and try to catch it,
To haul colours from sky and sea,
Tie them down to canvases – shreds of them,
Tattered edges – and take them back
In something that lasted forever.

❖ A Day in April

Twelve o'clock. She stands in the back porch,
Strands of gold hair tangling her face.
She calls his name; her voice is blown away.
He looks up nonetheless, as though he's heard
Somewhere deep inside. Light scours the hills,
Gullies of wind sweep back the shadow.
Fleet's heard her, flows down the field
In a bouncing waterfall of black and white.
She smiles. A lamb pities the air
With a cry as thin as milk. She turns inside.

He thuds the mud from his boots.
Has the mail come? Delivery from Hulberts?
The clock flickers softly in the hall;
Up in the landing window the blue of April
A rippling flag of sky –
This land is in his hands
As surely as it ran his father's.
At the table she rumbles the potatoes from the pan,
Looks at him with soft eyes. I've good news, she
    murmurs.

GAELIC

It lies in pockets in the hills,
A wink of gold that has not been panned
From the older veins and worn faces.

And sometimes on a dark river of night
I imagine it returning from the seas in its struggle
Like salmon to the birthright of the springs.

◈ Twelve O'Clock

Six boots tramp like hooves at the back door,
Come in to the room's warm glare, the ready table.

Pieces of broken talk, a folded newspaper, scraped
  chairs;
Grace a scattering of words, a murmur of amens.

Then split potatoes, soft and flowery, for bits of
  butter,
And poured glasses full of sudden sunlight,

As light slides out from late September cloud,
Glinting the knives, rosing the turned faces –

No sound except the somewhere song of a tap's drip
And down the hall a radio left talking to itself.

◈ SNATCHES OF SONG

Eight goldfinches,
Strung out along the telegraph wires
One October morning of gale:
Notes in the storm's tune.

◈ The Long Silence

On Iona the last Gaelic speaker has died.
This winter when the gales battled each roof and
    window
He was blown out and into the wind.

Once upon a time he was a tall man,
Leaning at the porch of his weaver's cottage,
His eyes like pools of the sea.

Now in the summer when the tourists come
You will hear the languages fast and loud –
But never a word of Gaelic there.

All over the western islands, they are vanishing
Like candles tonight, falling across the wind,
Their last words lost and drowned in time.

But everyone is talking, busy talking,
The radios and televisions are loud all night –
And no-one is listening to the long silence.

◈ A Poem for Ivars

A picture of Latvia:
You as a boy lifting potatoes behind a horse,
Swallows ticking wings in a farmyard sky,
The generals of winter a day yet closer.

In the hungry faces, the simple hands,
And this hard road through the furrows of Moscow,
I see richer earth still living, wooden songs
That could pull your people's faith.

If a man should come now to your door
Selling motorways, a rustle of money in his eyes;
Do not buy his road, for it leads
To all our lost riches, our need of God.

⬧ SEEING

The first time I saw them I was only three.
My father curled me out of bed,
Hoisted me on rounded shoulders
Up to the silver dark of the attic.
I was still nine-tenths asleep, in a far away
That furred my words and thoughts.

The dusty shadows of boxes and carpets and trains.
I heard the house gurgle and hiss;
Smelled the apples, moist and soft in their wrapped
    silence.

He held me high to the angled window,
Up into the fork of the roof.
I looked, searching,
For what he might want me to find.

Only the stars crackled and sparked
Above the grey shapes of the gardens.
The wind shifted restless in the trees.

Then something else, things
Swimming, hunching from the north,
Their underwings sheened in moonlight,
Beating that midnight in waves – fifty, a hundred,
    more –
Deep through the water of our sky, passing at last
Into someone else's night.

I followed them with my finger,
Knowing this is why I was there;
My father down below, beseeching me –
Did you see them? Did you see the geese?

◈ PEGGY

Peggy was big as a hillside –
Blue eyes piercing her face in pools of loch water,
Her Highland voice rising and falling, haunting and
    soft.
Everyone that came to visit had to work for her –
Fetch and carry, light fires, make beds –
She was a general in charge of her troops.
But at night by the hot pipes of her stove
She sat throned, the blue eyes dancing that round
    face,
The wisps of wild hair grey about it.
When she laughed, all of her rocked and rocked, still
    a girl,
And her face crinkled with delight.
She worked every day but the Sabbath –
Then only the clock kept time, nothing else moved,
And her guests went to church religiously.

After her stroke we visited her one last time;
She was a crab clawing at things –
She'd lost her balance, had toppled over,
Only the tears ran down the side of her that worked.
I was frightened, wanted back
The Peggy I'd known each summer –
Kind as a whole glen, generous as a harvest.

CALF

Born with everything but breath
He slid into the world a month too soon.

The trees traced with snow, the farm white-roofed,
Even the tractor buried useless.

The far mountains gullied white,
Lost under an avalanche of cloud.

And the calf nothing more than a flow of soft water,
Eyes thin against the light.

Carried like a slack brown sack
Out over the crackling field.

❖ EASTER ROSS

Still a shivering of snow in the hills
And a field of peewits
In black and white blinkings.

They rise, half a hundred,
Then another wave, and more
Until the whole air is made of peewits.

Their gracenotes blow away
Frail things making beautiful the blue light
This morning, this February day.

◈ THEN

We rattled and thumped across Mull, baggage and
    boxes and talk
In the beginning of April. Springtime was coming
    alive,
Creeping up through the cracks in the rocks
In daffodils, like the bright waving of children.
Now the skies glowered like the devil, rain clattered
Black and glassy over the windscreen, huge winds
Lifted hills into mist and dragoned the waves to
    silver.
Out in the water, caught between greens and blues
Between jags of rocks, an otter showed off
In a playground of impossible somersaults, was
    gone.
Then, from the dark heart of the thunderheads,
Down at the end of the island where the Atlantic
    truly begins,
A blessing of light showered from an invisible hand,
Turned golden the ocean in a Midas touch,
That single moment of our lives.

◈ SOME JUNE DAY

We will drive there some June day
To the furthest place west where the shell sand
Stretches in white miles till it turns to sky.
You'll take off your shoes and splash the shallows,
Joy in the flickering of fish, the dance of crabs;
You'll take my hand and tell me we should run
Fast as we can, fast till we lose our breath. And I,
    believing,
Will run with you, will laugh too, because of this –
The summer and the blue, the sudden lightness of
    the world
Upon our shoulders. Slowly we'll come back, still out
    of breath,
Drive towards evening to the village for wine and
    shellfish –
Soft salty lips of the Atlantic –
As a huge orange moon
Peels piece by piece across the sea.

◈ A GIFT

Today I saw three foals running;
There was no reason for them to play
With the summer morning, nothing
But the sheer exuberance of their hooves
In the warm green field,
And wanting the wind in their manes,
The curiosity of the skies, flickering
From thunderings of shadow to wild brightness.
Summer will run out, will fail and fall
Into the long and gusty lanes of blown-down
    autumn,
But the foals do not care
For today it will always be summer.

◈ THE STRANGER

All winter he braved the barn, took
The scuffings from our breadboard, the pecks
Meant for sparrows.
He'd come to work with wood, he said,
And brought us a table smelling still of cherry
From a tree blown down in mid-November storm.
The lambs nibbled the air about him, curious,
Let him touch their thin, milky bleats
With the big softness of his hands.
We eyed him, hovering,
Through the slats of the wood, awed
And wondering. When he made mud doves,
Cupped them in his hand and let them fly –
Laughed like a whole field of sunlight.

◈ FRILSHAM

We go to break bread and drink wine
In the early March sunlight of morning.

A church so old its walls might once have grown
Like strange stone roots up from the ground itself.

The story is a woman fled here once, so long ago
Her life is thin as parchment, was whispered down –

A few frail fragments from daughter to daughter.
She found water in the earth, a pure source

That gave healing. The water sang out of deep
    earth –
A living thing, full of the mystery of God.

Eight souls go to the communion rail,
Slow and old and grey.

Light falls in a golden cup:
Blesses their heads where they kneel.

I go outside, into the day where the yellow daffodils
    are breaking
In a jostling of young and yellow heads

And I hear it, I hear it clearly –
The bright chink, the jewellery, of spring water.

◈ GATHERING

Late in October we drove out for chestnuts,
The land hugged in mist, fouled by filthy streams
Chattering nonsense down fields and ditches.

We went by back roads,
By sudden farms that shone out gold
Until the tree.

I crouched under the fence, down into a deep
Smelling of earth and wet,
My feet scruffling thick browns of leaves.

Chestnut shells around me, broken open;
Some still lying intact like green helmets,
An edge of sheer mahogany gleaming from within.

I held them, dropped them into pockets,
Heard them land, their ovals making
A deep and woody knocking.

Back home I rolled them out
As pirates once poured pearls.

◈ REBECCA

We had coffee at Joe's, our elbows leaning
Over the red plastic of the takeaway tables.
She came from the thumb of Michigan, a green land
Reaching long into the lake. She'd come here to
    study books –
To the dead centre of the state – treeless and grey,
From a childhood of horses. She drew them for me –
Their dusty manes in the hot sweat of August
When sunlight honeycombed the stables. Foals
That were still, thin things on stilts,
Learning what to do with all that height.
Amish men coming to buy old horses that had run
    their last,
On dark October days of apples and fallen leaves.
Everything was horses. Now she was going home,
    she said,
And her eyes smiled blue. I was left in Joe's,
    listening,
To music going nowhere, to lots and lots of talk.

THE FERRYMAN

The blue ribbon of a river, too deep to ford,
a great chattering of water a hundred feet across,
and on the far bank a cottage fluttering smoke.

No-one crosses here without the ferryman's consent:
king or commoner, all are in the same boat –
thirty years he's criss-crossed the river for the one
    coin,

a coin for a crossing but for silence also:
the man who travels under cover of owls always
to meet the girl who is not his;

the boy who's running away,
whose eyes are full of ships and storms;
the priest who carries more than he came for.

That coin is worth its weight in gold,
to seal the slip of a tongue,
the spread scent of a secret.

So he has learned to say nothing,
the man with the bracken hair and the big hands –
to let out no more than where the best trout lie.

◈ In Grand Marais

The biggest lake in the world. May.
We hunch the shore as driven waves
Card the sand and stones. No agates,
Only hands left red and raw, held clenched in
    pockets.
The car hums a back road out of Grand Marais
And all at once signs for a museum, an agate house.
It looks asleep, its windows shut like eyes,
But then a shadow beckoning us round the back.
We slush the grass, curve past
A boat taller than us both, once blue, left chipped
    and dry.
The woman's on the step, all smudged with paint;
She's busy, could we come back tomorrow?
No. Sorry. She reads the disappointment in my eyes,
Vanishes, returns a moment later bearing
An old wooden box with a single leather strap.
I sit beside her on the doorstep;
She brings out agates from Mexico, Brazil and China,
From every secret cavern in the world:
Dragon eyes – flame-ringed, translucent, cut and
    loved –
Shining like strange and priceless moons.
I sit on that doorstep in Grand Marais
And catch sometimes the rough weather of her face,
And think of her own journey, the places she was
    beached
Before being washed up here, on the shores of Lake
    Superior,

Where winter's six feet deep and summer's boarded
    up
By late September. And I think too, as I sit beside her,
Sharing stones and stories, four thousand miles
    from home –
This is what being human means so much.

THE SOMEWHERE ROAD

The car hummed out the dirt track west
And the sun was low, a ball of orange-pink
Flickering the trees and fields,
Peaching soft the level land, painting the sudden
  somewhere of a house,
Stranded in a field, deep in a sea of grass.

And every house was still a story, and in the undug
  fields
Were books, whole tomes, untouched, unwritten –
Yet I could see their edges, in stray geese and bob-
  tailed deer,
And in the eyes of those who stopped beside the road
To smile, their faces made of light.

THE STRANGEST GIFT

Sister Mary Teresa gave me a wasps' nest from the
    convent garden –
Just the startings, the first leaves, a cocoon of
    whisperings –
Made out of thousands of buzzings.
To think that these yellow-black thugs
Could make such finery, such parchment,
A whole home telling the story of their days,
Written and wrought so perfect
Stung me, remembering how I'd thumped them
With thick books, reduced them to squashes on
    walls,
Nothing more than broken bits on carpets.
This little bowl, this bit of beginning
Rooted out by the gardener, reminds me
Of something bigger I keep choosing to forget,
About what beauty is, and where that beauty's found.

◈ FOR A BIRD

We found that fledgling on a back road, late
A ball of feathers, motionless and frail –
A blue-tit fallen from the nest, the weight
Of just a penny piece, that sky-blue tail
As soft as silk. I cupped it to the car
In cloths and paper towels; it sat the miles
Head bent as though in prayer. It seemed so far
Until at last from there behind the dials
I crept with that bright bundle on my knee
And brought it then so careful on its bed
To our old vet. He didn't say a word
But held it gentle to the light to see.
This little soul won't make it now, he said,
And we stood dumb, as though we hadn't heard.

◈ Songs

In the springtime he snags them
On the hillside above the village.

In the blue breeze they blow into his nets:
Finches and larks and linnets,

Beaks no larger than twigs
With songs bigger than whole cathedrals

Weighing no more than wind –
Little miracles that flock the air

In browns and reds and golds.
He rattles the road to the city

Sells them in bunches
To people who live on fourteenth floors

Who have known no song in all their lives,
Who will keep them in cages

Where neither spring nor sky will shine again.

◈ INVERGOWRIE

From far away
The thin blue notes of a curlew

Trailing over miles of sand. The sea and sky
Are rubbed together in grey light, the sun

Glazes outwards like a sore eyeball.
A flight of nothings rise in a trail, calling,

Smudge into mist.
My footprints were going somewhere

But the water has smoothed them away
Softly, and I am neither here nor there.

I stop and listen, in the middle of my life,
To a morning, a beginning again.

❖ THE MUSIC

He got his tunes that way;
He heard them,
As though they were edges of wind,
As if he saw the notes
In the loud rattle of the storm,
In the darkness – coming out of nothing.
He listened for them, as though they were bees
In ones and twos to begin with,
Then a swarm, a black net, a mist.
He had to catch them in the bow of his fiddle,
He had to find them before they passed,
Were gone and lost forever.

Where did they come from, those notes?
It was as though they had been sent to find him
Through the rampaging of Atlantic gales,
Or else had blown off course
Like a ship's cargo, like a pirate treasure hold,
Had spilled onto St Kilda, into his hands,
Into the fiddle,
Till it was filled brimful.

He wrote none of them down.
He caught them when they came;
He caught them in the net of his listening,
Recognised and remembered them,
Stored them in his head as the others
Stored fish and birds for winter.
They lay in the dark of his head
Like gold in the depths of a cave.

They died with him too
The day his eyes glazed and their light
Failed and faded for ever. The tunes were blown out
And back into the wind.

❖ GEESE

This morning I caught them
Against the headlands of rain
Glowering in from the west;
Half a hundred twinklings
In the angry sky, a gust of somethings
Grey against the greyness.

And then they turned in one gust
To climb the April sky
North, becoming a sprinkling of snowflakes
Underlit, to rise into a single skein –
An arrowhead ploughing the wind.

And I knew them as geese and stood watching
Their homing for Iceland;
I stood in the first splinters of rain
Watching until they were gone
And with them all my winter.

◈ THAT YEAR

The plough hit a hollowness,
A missing thing whose sound stopped him,
Brought him to his knees,
His both hands dragging that wet blackness back.

A hole in the earth. Seven, and the last light
Honeyed from the west across the fields.
He heard his heart; lowered himself through the
    emptiness,
Dropped into the softness of a cave kept silent
Who knew how many hundred years.

His eyes saw only darkness, then slowly woke, found
    walls
Curving the place to a beehive, a cupped heart
Woven out of careful stone, shaped smooth to
    something
Whose name was buried with the hands that built it.

Yet all at once he knew what this had been;
The whispers, soft as candle flames, breathed his
    hearing,
A peace shone from the dark and welled his heart
So full he dragged the tangle of his hat away, stood
    bowed,
As somewhere up above the curlews flew their
    evensong.

◈ MAY

We were coming home
On a day that swung between sun and thunder.
Sometimes the road awoke and glistened,
The song of blackbirds in the open windows
Like wet splashes, warm and soft.
And as we drove those last hills
Something in my mother broke,
Opened like a wound.
She stopped the car, her face all glassy,
In the huge banging of the wind.

Against that whole May sky she cried
So small against the hills;
Because my father was not there,
Because they could not see, together,
That place where they watched the stonechats,
The whole year greening into summer –
Larches, birches and the lambs with catkin tails.
I sat hunched in the car, hearing the huge waves
That tore from her, for all the years they loved,
    and wondered –
Do we grow wise in grief,
And where do all its rivers go?

◆ Catching the Light

Sometimes it's about running to stand
In sunlight splayed through the forest;
To drink upwards the light, pure
Until you are filled. But you know as well as I do
There are days it is dark always;
You wander hopeless through storms of branches,
    lost,
Weary for rest. Yet this is faith –
Not burying the little light that is left
Inside, but firing the heart onwards
To the morning that lies hidden
Under the whole of the hills.

▣ THIS MORNING

A swan beat over the house,
A hundred feet high and flagging north.
It was the wings I heard, the echoed bellows
Of those huge white curves, strong enough
To crack a grown man's arm. The neck stretched out
A whole length longer than itself, so it seemed
That bird flew through water,
Beating the pale blue February sky
For somewhere it knew, somewhere it must.
I stood still below on the dirt grey road
Not knowing my direction, wondering where I was.

◈ THE NOVEMBERLAND

Something wonderful there is in coming home
A ragged, late November night,

Leaving town and entering a midnight black,
Rain splintering the glass.

Headlights dig from darkness two white beams,
Rendering the other outer world so huge,

The car panthering the lanes,
Tunnelling a dusk that's roofed with branches.

Furry paws of wind come and nudge the car,
The trees above all wave like soundless cries.

And then an owl, a padded softness of a thing,
Suddens the eyes, glides through light and vanishes.

Until a long hour afterwards, at last,
Home's amber cave floods whole the heart,

Tyres crackle gravel and the engine shudders still,
A crystalling of stars engulfs the sky –

And silence pours back in to fill the night.

◈ PICTURES OF ASSYNT

Do not come here to take photographs,
Things that snip sea and sky into squares.
How can the lens remember larksong,
Or the shutter take back the scent of orchids?

Black veils of scowling rain
Drag across the rubble of the hills;
But one shuddering of glory
Turns water lillies to sudden pearls –

And Suilven and Canisp, dead dinosaurs of
    volcanoes,
Roar their heads into light.
Let the eye filter these pictures instead
Through the dark room of the mind, into the pages
    of the heart.

THE LAST WOLF

The last wolf in Scotland is not dead
Only sleeping.

He is no shaggy dog story
In the corries and crags of Cairngorm.

He is never in danger of being killed,
But rather dying of neglect.

If the last wolf promised to renounce violence
He would be allowed to lie by any peat fire in
    Scotland.

But his paws keep the memories of battles
And there is smoke in the grey of his eyes.

He has waited here two hundred years and more
For a blizzard that might flay the summer

From our soft hands and old excuses.

▣ JOURNEY

One night the train took me no further than Stirling;
It was spring, a shiver of snow still lingering the hills.

I dug my way into the back of a taxi –
Tired, not wanting to talk the last miles home.

But the driver did. I had to lean forwards
To catch the rough edges of his words:

He'd been a miner
In the oldest pit in Scotland.

He missed it, he said, the cut and thrust of words
Down there in the dark –

The way men shaped their shout and banter
Deep in the shafts that gleamed and shone;

He missed it, he said –
One day the pit would open up again and he'd go
   back.

The air in the taxi filled
With his black-blue warmth of words.

And I realised he went back there every day
Still, to keep the place alive

Taking his passengers with him on the journey.
Outside the night went past as black as coal.

⬙ NOVEMBER

His medals chink like old dead moons against his
    jacket;
What is he doing now but killing time?

Outside, the wintering sun folds through the park –
A white eye that is cold and dead.

North Africa, that long red sun,
Downing in hot copper, night by suffering night.

Planes trailing smoke in black goodbyes,
Rattled from the skies by someone else's guns.

The bombs falling like kisses in the far-off skies –
Out of earshot, soft and gentle their caressing fires.

Half-sleepless darks in open trucks,
The crystalling of stars in blue-black night, the
    hissing desert wind.

And then the finding of the sea, the sudden thunder
    of a blue
That washed away their sins in water cruel cold.

What did he come back to but slumped and dusty
    towns,
Bitter and wanting thanks for killing Hitler.

He's been here since 1972, since both his legs
Broke rank and fled and left him half himself.

The girl with false blonde hair who smiles and does
    not mean it,
Comes three times a day to wipe the surface of his
    world.

She does not care where he has come from;
The road, tapped out in Morse, that's written in his
    hands.

But every night he brings the stories back, he
    breathes them real –
The battle for a Britain he believed in.

◈ THE SLIDE

We longed for the sharp crinkle of December stars,
That ghostly mist like cobwebs in the grass,
Ten degrees below zero.

After the snow came petalling from the skies,
Settled into a deep quilt, the frost
Diamonded the top, making a thick crust.

On the long descent of the lawn
We made our slide, planed the ground
Hour after hour till it smiled with ice.

At night we teetered out with buckets,
Rushed the buckets down the slide's length
In one black stain.

Next day the slide was lethal,
A curling glacier that shot us downhill
In a single hiss.

Even after the thaw greened our world again
The slide remained written in the grass
As long as our stories.

⬙ CATHERINE ANNE

On the first of December she wrote them slowly,
In her very best writing in front of the fire.

Her mother looked at her when she saw the page,
Narrow eyes with nothing in them:

If you're a bad girl
All of your wishes will simply be burnt.

On the morning of the fourth she padded glittering
    flags,
For a basket of eggs from the barn's warm dark.

One slipped –
Smacked the stones in an orange splash.

On the twentieth she forgot she wasn't to sing
But read only the Bible and *The Pilgrim's Progress*.

On the twenty-third she put her elbows on the
    table.
On the twenty-fourth she did nothing

But carry in logs and eat her greens,
Wipe her boots and greet Mrs Dawson.

At two in the morning she creaked downstairs,
The moon globed in the sitting-room window.

And there it hung, high by the clock;
One of her own, red and fat.

She reached inside with the ghost of a smile –
A stocking full of ashes.

◈ MRS JAMES

Once a week I go for logs
To the old rectory at the end of the street.

She does not need the wood, she says,
She has not used the room or lit the fire

Since 1956. When I carry up the logs
She tells me how she had to work from six to
    midnight

In the war, how the south of England suffered,
How her brother was among the first to enter
    Belsen,

How he came back like a shadow of himself
And never spoke of it again.

Now her house is fast asleep. Not
In our world; it smells still of the 1930s:

Dead petals on the windowsills, dust
Dancing in the air where sunlight

Falls in slats from the high windows.
She is caught in her own war

To remember and preserve those days
Like butterflies, like pressed flowers, like
    leaves.

Every time I go for logs I enter
The great stopped clock of her house,

And breathe, a little afraid, a little thrilled
The stories that are written in the air,

Then go down softly for the logs her brother stacked
Forty years ago, the day before he died.

THE FARMER'S WIFE

She is distantly related
To someone my mother knows.

Sunlight bright as daffodils blows in
Over headlands ringing with birds.

I make my way through what used to be a garden
And now is nothing more than another beach –

A tide of old boxes, chicken wire and children's toys,
Washed up year by year and cluttered by the wind.

I knock softly on the back door;
A gust of dogs, bouncing and barking,

Flurries out from the house.
Then she's there

Shading her eyes against the sudden sun and
       smiling –
We shake hands.

The tousled grey of her hair,
Blue eyes, that wide smile.

No, she's not related to my mother's friend directly
But by her husband.

He died thirty years ago, she says,
And a wave catches her off-guard –

Her eyes melt against the sun
And her voice buckles.

❖ THE JOURNEY

That is not what I remember:
For me the dark watchfulness of strangers,
The tiredness of towns
Full of their own emptiness,
The desire to keep our journey secret as our
    gifts.

The morning we arrived
I smelled oranges in the fields,
The sun rose through the mist in a disc of
    gold,
Our sore feet scuffed the stubbled fields
And a blind man sang all alone
In the middle of the nowhere of the streets.

They were asleep too when we came,
One dusty beam of sun lancing the floor;
They were a painting already, their story
Frozen in the stone of legend –
Stranger than itself, yet made
Of nothing but its own simplicity.

We had thought God above all this
And we were wrong. We went home
Confused, following no star, wondering
Where we were going. I lay at night
Seeing the eyeless socket of the moon
Watching the vast emptiness of the dark,
Unblinking. It was in the beggars,

The sore emptiness of hunger in the homes we
    passed,
I saw my blindness.

That was the beginning of the journey.

◈ WINTER LIGHT

to come through a low blue door
under the high grey wall of a forgotten garden
into a place in winter, roofed by grey sky
the scattered holly berries of a robin's song

nothing is alive yet, all is deep and dark
wintered and fastened, shut into the earth
a book unopened, the whole story of the year
asleep, unwritten, underneath my feet

a door in the low sky opens, sunlight
struggles to silver the ground and fades;
soft things of rain whisper and nod and sing
this is enough, this is all I ask

◈ HEBRIDES

This shattered place, this place of fragments,
A play of wind and sea and light,
Shifting always, becoming and diminishing;
Out of nowhere the full brightness of morning
Blown away, buried and lost.

And yet, if you have faith, if you wait long enough,
There will be the miracle of an otter
Turning water into somersaults;
The jet blackness of a loch brought back to life
By the sudden touch of sun.

But you will take nothing home with you
Save your own changedness,
And this wind that will waken you
Sometimes, all your life, yearning to return.